Building AI Websites:

A Comprehensive Guide

Deepak Solanki

Daiso Publishing House
SKU: 250DAISO
BPDN: RS/145215/2023/2050

Note: The SKU (Stock Keeping Unit) and BPDN (Book Publishing Document Number) are unique identifiers used by the publisher for internal tracking and inventory purposes. The copyright notice indicates that the book is protected by copyright law and that any unauthorized reproduction, storage, or transmission of its contents is prohibited without permission from the publisher.

Disclaimer

The information and content provided in this book are for educational and informational purposes only. While the author has made every effort to ensure that the information provided is accurate and up-to-date, the author makes no representations or warranties of any kind, express or implied, about the completeness, accuracy, reliability, suitability, or availability with respect to the information and content contained in this book for any purpose.

The author disclaims any liability for any loss or damage whatsoever arising from the use of this book, its content, or the information provided. The reader is responsible for their own actions and decisions based on the information and content provided in this book.

Any examples of AI website development techniques or tools used in this book are not an endorsement of any specific product or service. The author does not have any commercial relationship with any of the products or services mentioned in this book.

The views and opinions expressed in this book are those of the author and do not necessarily reflect the official policy or position of any organization, employer, or company mentioned in this book.

The author has taken all reasonable care to ensure that the information and content provided in this book do not infringe on any intellectual property rights or other rights of any third party. If any infringement has inadvertently occurred, the author will make every effort to correct the error as soon as possible upon notification.

All trademarks mentioned in this book belong to their respective owners and are used for identification purposes only. No endorsement or sponsorship by the trademark owners is implied or intended.

Preface

In recent years, we have witnessed an explosion in the amount of data being generated across industries. With this deluge of data, there has been a growing interest in leveraging Artificial Intelligence (AI) to process and analyze this data, and to derive valuable insights. One area where AI has been making significant strides is in website development. AI-powered websites are becoming more prevalent, and are being used by organizations to deliver better user experiences, personalize content, and increase engagement.

In this book, we will explore the world of AI-powered websites, and provide a comprehensive guide on how to build and deploy them. We will cover a wide range of topics, including the different types of AI models for website development, best practices for training and fine-tuning AI models, integrating AI models into websites, creating user interfaces for AI-powered features, testing and refining AI websites, and monitoring and maintaining the AI models and websites.

The book is divided into several sections, each covering a specific aspect of AI website development. In the first section, we will provide an overview of website development technologies, and introduce the different types of AI models that can be used to power websites. We will discuss the advantages and disadvantages of each model, and provide examples of how they can be used in real-world scenarios.

The second section will focus on creating and training AI models. We will provide a step-by-step guide on how to create and train AI models for website development, and discuss best practices for selecting and preparing training data. We will also provide guidance on how to fine-tune the model for better results, and discuss common pitfalls and challenges in this process.

The third section will cover integrating AI models into websites, and creating user interfaces for AI-powered features. We will discuss the different methods for integrating AI models into websites, and provide guidance on how to create user interfaces that are intuitive and user-friendly.

In the fourth section, we will cover testing and refining AI websites. We will discuss best practices for testing AI websites, and provide guidance on how to identify and fix common errors and issues. We will also discuss the importance of ongoing monitoring and maintenance of AI models and websites.

In the fifth and final section, we will discuss the future of AI website development. We will explore emerging trends in AI website development, potential future applications of AI in website development, and the challenges and opportunities for AI website developers.

Acknowledgement

I would like to express my heartfelt gratitude to my mother, who has been a constant source of support and encouragement throughout my life. Her unwavering love and guidance have been instrumental in shaping the person I am today, and I am eternally grateful for her presence in my life.

I would also like to thank Daiso Publication House for giving me the opportunity to share my knowledge and insights on AI website development with readers around the world. Their professionalism, expertise, and dedication to quality have been invaluable in helping me bring this book to fruition.

I would like to thank all the readers who have chosen to invest their time and resources in reading this book. I hope that the information and insights contained herein will be useful and valuable to you, and I welcome any feedback or comments you may have.

Deepak Solanki

Contents

Introduction

Artificial intelligence (AI) is a rapidly growing field that has the potential to revolutionize many industries, including website development. In this article, we'll explore the applications of AI in website development and the benefits it can provide.

✓ Understanding AI for Website Development

Before we dive into the applications of AI in website development, let's take a moment to understand what AI is and how it works.

AI is a branch of computer science that focuses on the development of intelligent machines that can perform tasks that would normally require human intelligence, such as learning, reasoning, problem-solving, and decision-making. AI systems can be trained to recognize patterns in data, make predictions, and automate routine tasks.

In website development, AI can be used to automate tasks that would normally require human intervention, such as content creation, user analysis, and customer support. AI can also be used to personalize website content for individual users, making the user experience more engaging and relevant.

✓ Applications of AI in Website Development

1. Personalization

One of the most significant applications of AI in website development is personalization. AI can be used to personalize website content for individual users based on their behavior, preferences, and past interactions with the website.

For example, an AI-powered website can analyze a user's browsing behavior and recommend content that is relevant to their interests. This can include product recommendations, blog articles, or other types of content.

Personalization can significantly improve the user experience by making the website more engaging and relevant to the user's needs. It can also increase user engagement and conversion rates by presenting users with content that is tailored to their interests and preferences.

2. Chatbots

Another popular application of AI in website development is the use of chatbots. Chatbots are AI-powered conversational interfaces that can interact with users in natural language.

Chatbots can be used to provide customer support, answer user questions, and automate routine tasks. For example, a chatbot can be used to provide users with answers to common questions, such as shipping and return policies.

Chatbots can significantly improve the user experience by providing users with quick and efficient access to information and support. They can also reduce the workload of customer support teams by handling routine inquiries and tasks.

3. Image and Video Recognition

AI can also be used to recognize and tag images and videos on a website. This can make it easier for users to search for and find the content they're looking for.

For example, an AI-powered website can analyze images and videos and tag them with relevant keywords. This can make it easier for users to find the content they're looking for by searching for keywords.

Image and video recognition can significantly improve the user experience by making it easier for users to find relevant content on the website. It can also reduce the workload of content creators by automating the tagging process.

4. Recommendation Engines

Another application of AI in website development is the use of recommendation engines. Recommendation engines use AI algorithms to analyze user behavior and recommend relevant content or products.

For example, an AI-powered e-commerce website can analyze a user's browsing and purchase history and recommend products that are relevant to their interests. This can improve user engagement and conversion rates by presenting users with products that are tailored to their preferences.

Recommendation engines can significantly improve the user experience by presenting users with content or products that are relevant to their interests. They can also increase user engagement and conversion rates by presenting users with personalized recommendations.

5. Natural Language Processing (NLP)

AI-powered natural language processing (NLP) can be used to analyze and interpret user language. This allows websites to better understand and respond to user needs.

✓ Importance of building an AI website

In today's fast-paced digital world, businesses and organizations are constantly seeking new ways to enhance their online presence and improve user experiences. One of the most effective ways to achieve this is by building an AI website. An AI website uses artificial intelligence to enhance its functionality and provide users with personalized experiences. In this article, we'll explore the importance of building an AI website and the benefits it can provide.

1. Personalization

One of the most significant benefits of building an AI website is the ability to provide personalized experiences to users. By analyzing user behavior and preferences, an AI website can tailor its content and offerings to each individual user.

Personalization can greatly enhance the user experience by providing users with content that is relevant to their interests and needs. This can increase engagement, encourage repeat visits, and ultimately lead to greater customer satisfaction and loyalty.

2. Enhanced User Engagement

Building an AI website can also greatly enhance user engagement. By providing personalized experiences and tailoring content to each user's preferences, an AI website can make the user experience more engaging and enjoyable.

For example, an AI website may use machine learning algorithms to recommend products or services based on a user's browsing history. By doing so, the website can offer users products or services that are more likely to interest them, which can increase the likelihood of a purchase.

Additionally, an AI website can also offer interactive features, such as chatbots or virtual assistants, which can provide users with instant feedback and support. This can greatly enhance the user experience by providing a more human-like interaction and improving user satisfaction.

3. Improved Customer Service

An AI website can also greatly improve customer service by offering instant support and assistance to users. Chatbots or virtual assistants can be used to answer common questions, resolve issues, or provide product recommendations.

By offering instant support, an AI website can reduce the workload on customer service teams, freeing up resources to focus on more complex issues. This can also greatly improve customer satisfaction by providing users with instant access to support when they need it.

4. Increased Efficiency

Building an AI website can also greatly increase efficiency. By automating routine tasks, an AI website can reduce the workload on human staff and improve overall productivity.

For example, an AI website may use machine learning algorithms to analyze user data and make predictions about future trends or customer behavior. This can help businesses to make more informed decisions and allocate resources more effectively.

Additionally, an AI website can also automate repetitive tasks, such as data entry or content creation. This can save time and resources, allowing human staff to focus on more complex and strategic tasks.

5. Competitive Advantage

Building an AI website can also provide businesses with a competitive advantage. By offering personalized experiences, instant support, and improved efficiency, an AI website can differentiate itself from competitors and attract more customers.

In today's fast-paced digital world, businesses that fail to adapt to changing technologies risk falling behind their competitors. By building an AI website, businesses can stay ahead of the curve and offer users the latest and most advanced technology available.

6. Cost Savings

Building an AI website can also result in significant cost savings for businesses. By automating routine tasks and reducing the workload on human staff, an AI website can reduce labor costs and increase overall efficiency.

Additionally, an AI website can also help businesses to make more informed decisions, which can lead to cost savings in the long run. By analyzing user data and making predictions about future trends, businesses can make more accurate and informed decisions about where to allocate resources and how to market their products or services.

In this book, readers will learn how to leverage artificial intelligence to enhance their online presence and improve user experiences. The book will provide a comprehensive overview of the different types of AI, their applications in website development, and best practices for integrating AI components into a website.

The book will be divided into several sections, including an introduction to AI and its applications in website development, the fundamentals of website development, building an AI website, ethics and governance considerations, future developments in AI and website development, and case studies and examples.

The introduction section will provide an overview of the history of AI, its current state, and its potential for future development. The section on website development will cover the fundamentals of web design principles, front-end and back-end development, and content management systems, as well as best practices for website development.

The section on building an AI website will focus specifically on integrating AI components into a website, such as chatbots, virtual assistants, and recommendation engines. It will cover how to collect and analyze user data to improve the functionality and personalization of an AI website, and provide guidance on how to choose the right algorithms and models for an AI website.

The section on ethics and governance will cover the ethical challenges posed by AI, such as bias and privacy concerns, and provide guidance on how to ensure an AI website is compliant with legal and regulatory frameworks.

The section on future developments in AI and website development will provide an overview of emerging technologies, such as quantum computing and blockchain, and their potential applications in website development. It will also cover emerging trends in AI and website development, such as the increasing use of AI in e-commerce and the integration of AI into the internet of things.

Throughout the book, case studies and examples will be used to illustrate the concepts and best practices covered in each section. These case studies will include real-world examples of AI websites, such as chatbots and recommendation engines, and how they have been used to improve user experiences and drive business outcomes.

In conclusion, the book will summarize the key takeaways and provide guidance on next steps for businesses and organizations looking to build an AI website. It will include recommendations for further reading and resources to help businesses and organizations stay up-to-date with the latest developments in AI and website development.

AI for Website Development

Artificial Intelligence (AI) has revolutionized many industries, and website development is no exception. AI and Machine Learning (ML) algorithms are being used to build more responsive, intelligent, and personalized websites that offer a better user experience. In this article, we will explore how AI and ML can be used in website development, and some of the benefits and challenges associated with these technologies.

What is Artificial Intelligence?

Artificial Intelligence refers to the ability of machines to perform tasks that typically require human intelligence, such as recognizing images, understanding natural language, and making decisions based on data. AI algorithms can learn from data and improve their performance over time, making them increasingly accurate and efficient.

AI can be divided into two main categories: narrow or weak AI and general or strong AI. Narrow AI refers to systems that are designed for specific tasks, such as image recognition or natural language processing. These systems can perform their tasks with a high degree of accuracy but are not capable of generalizing beyond their specific domain. General AI, on the other hand, refers to systems that are capable of performing a wide range of tasks and can learn from experience, much like a human being.

What is Machine Learning?

Machine Learning is a subfield of AI that is concerned with developing algorithms that can learn from data. ML algorithms can be trained on large datasets to recognize patterns and make predictions based on past data. For example, an ML algorithm can be trained to recognize faces in images by analyzing a large dataset of labeled images.

ML algorithms can be divided into three main categories: supervised learning, unsupervised learning, and reinforcement learning. In supervised learning, the algorithm is trained on a labeled dataset, where the correct output is provided for each input. The algorithm learns to map inputs to outputs based on the training data. In unsupervised learning, the algorithm is trained on an unlabeled dataset, and the goal is to discover patterns or structure in the data. In reinforcement learning, the algorithm learns through trial and error by interacting with an environment and receiving rewards or punishments based on its actions.

How AI and ML can be used in Website Development

AI and ML can be used in website development to enhance the user experience, automate routine tasks, and improve website performance. Here are some examples of how AI and ML are being used in website development:

1. Personalization

AI and ML can be used to personalize website content and recommendations based on user behavior and preferences. For example, an e-commerce website can use ML algorithms to recommend products based on a user's past purchases, search history, and browsing behavior. This can improve the user experience and increase conversion rates.

2. Chatbots

AI-powered chatbots can be used to provide 24/7 customer support and handle routine inquiries, freeing up human agents to focus on more complex issues. Chatbots can use natural language processing (NLP) to understand user queries and provide relevant responses. This can improve customer satisfaction and reduce response times.

3. Search

AI and ML can be used to improve website search functionality by providing more accurate and relevant results. For example, an e-commerce website can use ML algorithms to analyze user search queries and suggest relevant products based on user behavior and preferences.

4. Content Creation

AI and ML can be used to generate content for websites, such as product descriptions, news articles, and social media posts. Natural Language Generation (NLG) algorithms can analyze data and generate human-like text that is grammatically correct and semantically meaningful. This can save time and resources for website owners and improve the consistency and quality of content.

✓ The role of AI in website development

Artificial Intelligence (AI) has become a significant part of our daily lives, and it is changing the way we interact with technology. In recent years, AI has made significant advancements, and it is now being used in various industries, including website development. AI is being used in website development to make websites more user-friendly, efficient, and personalized. In this article, we will explore the role of AI in website development and the benefits it brings.

What is AI in Website Development?

AI refers to the ability of machines to perform tasks that typically require human intelligence, such as recognizing images, understanding natural language, and making decisions based on data. In website development, AI is being used to automate tasks, personalize content, and enhance the user experience.

AI algorithms can learn from data and improve their performance over time, making them increasingly accurate and efficient. AI can be used to analyze large amounts of data, generate insights, and make predictions. AI can also be used to automate routine tasks and improve website performance.

Role of AI in Website Development

AI is playing an increasingly significant role in website development, and it is being used in various ways. Here are some of the ways in which AI is being used in website development:

1. Personalization

One of the primary roles of AI in website development is personalization. AI algorithms can be used to personalize website content and recommendations based on user behavior and preferences. For example, an e-commerce website can use AI algorithms to recommend products based on a user's past purchases, search history, and browsing behavior. This can improve the user experience and increase conversion rates.

2. Chatbots

AI-powered chatbots are becoming increasingly popular in website development. Chatbots can be used to provide 24/7 customer support and handle routine inquiries, freeing up human agents to focus on more complex issues. Chatbots can use natural language processing (NLP) to understand user queries and provide relevant responses. This can improve customer satisfaction and reduce response times.

3. Search

AI can be used to improve website search functionality by providing more accurate and relevant results. For example, an e-commerce website can use AI algorithms to analyze user search queries and suggest relevant products based on user behavior and preferences.

4. Content Creation

AI can be used to generate content for websites, such as product descriptions, news articles, and social media posts. Natural Language Generation (NLG) algorithms can analyze data and generate human-like text that is grammatically correct and semantically meaningful. This can save time and resources for website owners and improve the consistency and quality of content.

5. Image Recognition

AI can be used to improve the accuracy and speed of image recognition on websites. For example, an e-commerce website can use AI algorithms to recognize product images and automatically tag them with relevant keywords. This can improve website search functionality and make it easier for users to find the products they are looking for.

✓ Benefits of AI in Website Development

The use of AI in website development offers many benefits, including:

1. Improved User Experience

The use of AI in website development can improve the user experience by providing personalized content, faster response times, and more accurate search results.

2. Increased Efficiency

AI can automate routine tasks and improve website performance, freeing up human resources to focus on more critical tasks.

3. Improved Customer Service

The use of AI-powered chatbots can improve customer service by providing 24/7 support and handling routine inquiries.

4. Reduced Costs

The use of AI in website development can reduce costs by automating routine tasks, such as content generation and image recognition.

✓ Examples of AI-powered websites

1. Netflix

Netflix is a streaming platform that uses AI algorithms to recommend content to its users. The platform analyzes user data, such as viewing history and search queries, to provide personalized recommendations. This has helped Netflix to improve user engagement and retention.

2. Spotify

Spotify is a music streaming platform that uses AI algorithms to recommend songs to its users. The platform analyzes user data, such as listening history and playlists, to provide personalized recommendations. This has helped Spotify to increase user engagement and retention.

3. Grammarly

Grammarly is a writing assistant that uses AI algorithms to improve writing quality. The platform analyzes text and provides suggestions for grammar, spelling, and punctuation. The platform also provides suggestions for sentence structure and word choice. This has helped Grammarly to become one of the most popular writing tools on the web.

4. The Grid

The Grid is a website builder that uses AI algorithms to design websites. The platform analyzes user content, such as images and text, and automatically designs a website based on the content. The Grid has helped to reduce the time and cost of website design for many users.

5. Zestful

Zestful is an employee recognition platform that uses AI algorithms to suggest rewards for employees. The platform analyzes employee data, such as performance metrics and work history, to provide personalized reward suggestions. This has helped to increase employee engagement and retention.

6. Hugging Face

Hugging Face is a chatbot platform that uses AI algorithms to create chatbots. The platform uses Natural Language Processing (NLP) algorithms to understand user queries and provide relevant responses. This has helped to reduce the time and cost of chatbot development for many users.

7. Pinterest

Pinterest is a social media platform that uses AI algorithms to recommend content to its users. The platform analyzes user data, such as pins and boards, to provide personalized recommendations. This has helped Pinterest to increase user engagement and retention.

8. Alibaba

Alibaba is an e-commerce platform that uses AI algorithms to provide personalized product recommendations to its users. The platform analyzes user data, such as search history and purchase history, to provide relevant product recommendations. This has helped Alibaba to increase user engagement and conversion rates.

9.   The North Face

The North Face is a clothing brand that uses AI algorithms to provide personalized recommendations to its customers. The brand uses a chatbot that analyzes customer data, such as location and weather, to provide recommendations for clothing and gear. This has helped The North Face to improve the user experience and increase sales.

Collecting and Preparing Data for AI Website Development

1. **Determine what data you need**: The first step in collecting and preparing data for AI website development is to determine what types of data you need. As mentioned earlier, user data, content data, and historical data are some of the types of data that are commonly required for AI website development.

2. **Collect the data**: Once you have determined what types of data you need, the next step is to collect the data. There are various ways to collect data, depending on the type of data you need. For example, you can collect user data using website analytics tools, surveys, and feedback forms. Content data can be collected through web scraping tools or by manual data entry. Historical data can be collected from various sources, such as databases, APIs, or web archives.

3. **Clean the data**: After collecting the data, it is important to clean and preprocess the data to ensure that it is accurate and consistent. This involves removing duplicates, fixing errors, and formatting the data in a standardized way. Data cleaning can be a time-consuming process, but it is crucial for ensuring that the AI algorithms can analyze the data effectively.

4. **Label the data**: Labeling the data involves adding descriptive tags or categories to the data, which can help the AI algorithms understand and analyze the data. For example, you might label content data with categories

like "product description," "blog post," or "news article." Labeling the data can be done manually or using automated tools like Natural Language Processing (NLP) algorithms.

5. **Organize the data**: Once the data is cleaned and labeled, it is important to organize the data in a way that makes it easy for the AI algorithms to access and analyze. This might involve storing the data in a database or a data management system. Organizing the data can also involve creating data pipelines or workflows that automate the process of collecting, cleaning, and labeling the data.

6. **Test the data**: Finally, it is important to test the data to ensure that it is accurate and effective for AI website development. This might involve running tests on the AI algorithms to see how well they perform with the data. Testing can help identify any issues or errors in the data and ensure that the AI algorithms are working correctly.

Here are some additional resources that can help with collecting and preparing data for AI website development:

- Google Analytics: https://analytics.google.com/

- SurveyMonkey: https://www.surveymonkey.com/

- BeautifulSoup: https://www.crummy.com/software/BeautifulSoup/

- OpenRefine: https://openrefine.org/

- Amazon Mechanical Turk: https://www.mturk.com/

- TensorFlow Data Validation:
  https://www.tensorflow.org/tfx/data_validation/

✓ Types of data required for AI website development

1. **User data**: User data refers to information about website visitors, such as their demographics, location, behavior, and preferences. This data is typically collected through website analytics tools like Google Analytics or through surveys and feedback forms. User data is essential for developing AI-powered website features like personalization and recommendation systems.

2. **Content data**: Content data refers to the content on a website, such as text, images, videos, and audio. This data is used by AI algorithms to analyze and categorize content, which can improve the accuracy of search results and recommendation systems. Content data can be collected through web scraping tools or by manual data entry.

3. **Historical data**: Historical data refers to data that is collected over time, such as website traffic, sales data, or social media activity. This data can be used to identify trends and patterns, which can help to improve website performance and user experience. Historical data can be collected from various sources, such as databases, APIs, or web archives.

4. **Environmental data**: Environmental data refers to external factors that can affect website performance, such as weather, traffic conditions, or events. This data can be used to optimize website content and advertising based on current conditions. Environmental data can be collected from various sources, such as weather APIs, traffic cameras, or event calendars.

5. **Sensor data**: Sensor data refers to data that is collected by sensors, such as temperature sensors, motion sensors, or sound sensors. This data can be used to improve website performance and user experience by providing real-time feedback and adjusting website features accordingly. Sensor data can be collected using IoT devices or specialized sensors.

6. **Transactional data**: Transactional data refers to data that is generated by user transactions, such as purchases, downloads, or sign-ups. This data can be used to improve website performance and user experience by providing personalized recommendations and tailored content. Transactional data can be collected using eCommerce platforms or CRM systems.

✓ **Data collection and preparation techniques**

Data collection and preparation are critical steps in AI website development. Without high-quality data, machine learning algorithms cannot be trained effectively, and AI-powered website features may not function as intended. In this guide, we will cover some of the key techniques for data collection and preparation, along with examples and resources to help you get started.

1. Web Scraping

Web scraping is the process of automatically extracting data from websites. This technique involves using software tools to crawl web pages, extract specific data points, and store them in a structured format. Web scraping can be used to collect a wide range of data, including product details, user reviews, and content.

For example, an e-commerce website could use web scraping to collect product details from competitor sites to inform pricing decisions. A news website could use web scraping to collect headlines and article summaries from other news sites to inform content curation.

There are many tools available for web scraping, including Python libraries like Beautiful Soup and Scrapy, as well as commercial tools like Octoparse and Parsehub. However, it is important to note that web scraping can be a legally gray area, and websites may have terms of service that prohibit or restrict scraping. Therefore, it is important to understand the legal and ethical considerations before scraping data from a website.

Useful links

- Web Scraping with Python: A Comprehensive Guide - https://www.scrapingbee.com/blog/web-scraping-python/

- Beautiful Soup Documentation - https://www.crummy.com/software/BeautifulSoup/bs4/doc/

- Scrapy Documentation - https://docs.scrapy.org/en/latest/

- Octoparse Homepage - https://www.octoparse.com/

- Parsehub Homepage - https://www.parsehub.com/

2. Data Cleaning

Data cleaning is the process of identifying and correcting errors in data. This step is crucial for ensuring that the data used in AI website development is accurate and reliable. Data cleaning may involve tasks like removing duplicate entries, filling in missing values, and correcting formatting errors.

For example, if an e-commerce website collects product data from multiple sources, it may need to clean and standardize the data to ensure that all products are listed consistently. This could involve removing duplicate products, filling in missing prices or descriptions, and standardizing units of measurement.

There are many tools and libraries available for data cleaning, including Python libraries like Pandas and OpenRefine. These tools can help automate common data cleaning tasks and make the process more efficient.

Useful links:

- Data Cleaning with Python: A Complete Guide

- Pandas Documentation

- OpenRefine Homepage

3. Data Normalization

Data normalization is the process of organizing data into a standard format that can be easily analyzed. This technique is particularly useful when working with data that comes from multiple sources or in different formats. Data normalization may involve tasks like converting text to numerical values or standardizing units of measurement.

For example, if an e-commerce website collects product data from multiple vendors, it may need to normalize the data to ensure that all products are listed consistently. This could involve converting product descriptions to a standardized format, such as using bullet points, and standardizing units of measurement for product dimensions.

There are many tools and libraries available for data normalization, including Python libraries like Pandas and NumPy. These tools can help automate common normalization tasks and make the process more efficient.

Useful links:

- Data Normalization with Python: A Complete Guide - https://towardsdatascience.com/data-normalization-with-python-scikit-learn-e18ddf2c5d2e

- NumPy Documentation - https://numpy.org/doc/stable/

4. Data Integration

Data integration involves combining data from multiple sources into a single dataset. This technique can be useful for identifying relationships between different data points and providing a more comprehensive view of the data.

For example, an e-commerce website may want to combine data on product sales with data on customer demographics to identify trends in purchasing behavior. This could involve integrating data from different sources, such as sales data from an e-commerce platform and demographic data from a third-party provider.

- Talend Data Integration - https://www.talend.com/products/data-integration/

- IBM InfoSphere DataStage - https://www.ibm.com/products/infosphere-datastage

- Apache NiFi - https://nifi.apache.org/

Data cleaning and preprocessing for machine learning

Data cleaning and preprocessing are crucial steps in machine learning, as they can greatly affect the accuracy and performance of the resulting model. Here are some common techniques used for data cleaning and preprocessing:

- **Handling missing values**: If the dataset contains missing values, there are several ways to handle them, including deleting the rows or columns with missing data, imputing the missing values with the mean or median, or using a more advanced imputation technique like K-nearest neighbors.

- **Handling outliers**: Outliers can be dealt with by removing them from the dataset, transforming them to more reasonable values, or using anomaly detection algorithms to identify and handle them.

- **Feature scaling and normalization**: This involves transforming the features to a common scale so that the values of different features can be compared more easily. Common methods include standardization, min-max scaling, and logarithmic scaling.

- **Encoding categorical variables**: Categorical variables need to be converted to numerical form before they can be used in machine learning models. Common techniques include one-hot encoding, label encoding, and ordinal encoding.

- **Feature selection and dimensionality reduction**: If the dataset contains too many features, it can lead to overfitting and reduced performance. Feature selection and dimensionality reduction techniques can be used to select the most relevant features or to reduce the dimensionality of the dataset.

- **Splitting the dataset**: Finally, the dataset needs to be split into training and testing sets to evaluate the performance of the model. Common techniques include random splitting, stratified splitting, and time-based splitting.

✓ **Step-by-step guide for data cleaning and preprocessing in machine learning:**

I. **Identify and handle missing data**: The first step is to identify if the dataset contains any missing values. There are several ways to handle missing data, such as deleting the rows or columns with missing data, imputing the missing values with the mean or median, or using a more advanced imputation technique like K-nearest neighbors. Here is a detailed guide on how to handle missing data: https://towardsdatascience.com/how-to-handle-missing-data-8646b18db0d4

II. **Identify and handle outliers**: The next step is to identify if the dataset contains any outliers. Outliers can be dealt with by removing them from the dataset, transforming them to more reasonable values, or using anomaly detection algorithms to identify and handle them. Here is a guide on outlier detection techniques: https://towardsdatascience.com/a-brief-overview-of-outlier-detection-techniques-1e0b2c19e561

III. **Feature scaling and normalization**: This involves transforming the features to a common scale so that the values of different features can be compared more easily. Common methods include standardization, min-max scaling, and logarithmic scaling. Here is a guide on feature scaling and normalization: https://towardsdatascience.com/normalization-vs-standardization-quantitative-analysis-a91e8a79cebf

IV. **Encoding categorical variables**: Categorical variables need to be converted to numerical form before they can be used in machine learning models. Common techniques include one-hot encoding, label encoding, and ordinal encoding. Here is a guide on encoding categorical_variables: https://towardsdatascience.com/categorical-encoding-using-label-encoding-and-one-hot-encoder-911ef77fb5bd

V. **Feature selection and dimensionality reduction:** If the dataset contains too many features, it can lead to overfitting and reduced performance. Feature selection and dimensionality reduction techniques can be used to select the most relevant features or to reduce the dimensionality of the dataset. Here is a guide on feature selection and dimensionality reduction: https://towardsdatascience.com/feature-selection-techniques-in-machine-learning-with-python-f24e7da3f36e

VI.   **Splitting the dataset**: Finally, the dataset needs to be split into training and testing sets to evaluate the performance of the model. Common techniques include random splitting, stratified splitting, and time-based splitting. Here is a guide on splitting the dataset: https://towardsdatascience.com/train-test-split-and-cross-validation-in-python-80b61beca4b6

Building an AI Model for Website Development:

Step-by-step guide to building an AI model for website development:

1. **Choose the type of AI model**: There are various types of AI models that can be used for website development, such as classification models, regression models, clustering models, and recommendation systems. Choose the model that best fits your website's requirements.

2. **Collect and prepare data**: Before you can build an AI model, you need to collect and prepare the data that will be used to train the model. This may involve gathering data from various sources, cleaning the data, and formatting it so that it can be used for machine learning.

3. **Choose an AI framework**: Once you have your data, you need to choose an AI framework to build your model. Some popular frameworks include TensorFlow, PyTorch, and Scikit-learn. Each framework has its own strengths and weaknesses, so choose the one that best suits your needs.

4. **Define the model architecture**: The next step is to define the architecture of your AI model. This involves determining the number of layers, the number of

neurons in each layer, and the activation functions to be used.

5. **Train the model**: Once you have defined the architecture, you need to train the model using your prepared data. This involves feeding the data into the model and adjusting the weights and biases to minimize the error between the predicted outputs and the actual outputs.

6. **Fine-tune the model**: After training the model, you may need to fine-tune it to improve its performance. This could involve adjusting the learning rate, adding regularization, or tweaking the model architecture.

7. **Deploy the model on a website**: Once your model is trained and fine-tuned, you can deploy it on a website. This may involve integrating the model with your website's backend code and creating a user interface for the AI-powered features.

Some helpful resources for each step:

1. Types of AI models for website development: https://www.analyticsvidhya.com/blog/2018/05/essentials-of-deep-learning-trudging-into-unsupervised-deep-learning/

2. Collecting and preparing data for machine learning: https://towardsdatascience.com/data-preprocessing-concepts-fa946d11c825

3. Choosing an AI framework: https://builtin.com/artificial-intelligence/machine-learning-frameworks

4. Defining the model architecture:
   https://towardsdatascience.com/understanding-neural-networks-19020b758230

5. Training the model:
   https://towardsdatascience.com/machine-learning-basics-part-3-9d690cba9b34

6. Fine-tuning the model:
   https://towardsdatascience.com/hyperparameter-tuning-c5619e7e6624

7. Deploying the model on a website:
   https://towardsdatascience.com/how-to-deploy-a-machine-learning-model-on-the-web-97441d56f379

✓ Types of AI models for website development

There are several types of AI models that can be used for website development, depending on the specific use case and goals of the website. Here are some common types of AI models:

- **Rule-based systems**: These AI models are based on a set of pre-defined rules and logical statements. They are generally used for simple tasks and decision-making processes, such as chatbots or virtual assistants.

- **Supervised learning models**: These AI models are trained on labeled data sets to recognize patterns and make predictions or classifications. They are commonly used for tasks such as image or speech recognition, recommendation systems, and sentiment analysis.

- **Unsupervised learning models**: These AI models are used to identify patterns and relationships in unlabeled data sets. They are commonly used for tasks such as clustering, anomaly detection, and feature extraction.

- **Reinforcement learning models**: These AI models learn by interacting with an environment and receiving feedback in the form of rewards or penalties. They are commonly used for tasks such as game playing, robotics, and autonomous vehicles.

- **Deep learning models**: These AI models use artificial neural networks to process complex data inputs and learn from them. They are commonly used for tasks such as natural language processing, image and speech recognition, and autonomous decision-making.

✓ Creating and training the AI model

Creating and training an AI model for website development involves several steps:

1. **Define the problem and gather data**: The first step is to define the problem you want to solve with your AI model. For example, you may want to create a recommendation system that suggests products to users based on their browsing history. Once you have defined your problem, you need to gather relevant data. This data should be labeled and representative of the real-world scenarios the model will encounter.

2. **Choose a model architecture:** Based on the problem you are trying to solve and the type of data you have, you can choose an appropriate model architecture. For example, if you are working with image data, you may choose a convolutional neural network (CNN), while if you are working with text data, you may choose a recurrent neural network (RNN) or a transformer model.

3. **Preprocess and clean the data**: To ensure the accuracy and effectiveness of the AI model, you need to preprocess and clean the data. This involves removing duplicates, handling missing values, and transforming

the data into a suitable format for training the model. You may also need to perform feature engineering to extract relevant features from the data.

4. **Train the model:** Once the data is prepared, you can train the AI model using a variety of techniques such as gradient descent, backpropagation, or Bayesian optimization. This involves selecting appropriate hyperparameters and tuning the model to improve its accuracy. You may also need to split the data into training, validation, and test sets to evaluate the model's performance.

5. **Validate the model**: After training the model, you need to validate its performance using a separate validation set of data. This will help you identify any overfitting or underfitting issues and fine-tune the model accordingly. You may need to adjust the model architecture or hyperparameters to improve its performance.

6. **Evaluate the model:** Finally, you need to evaluate the performance of the AI model using a test set of data. This will help you determine how well the model will perform in real-world scenarios and identify any further areas for improvement. You may need to iterate on the previous steps to improve the model's performance.

TensorFlow: https://www.tensorflow.org/

TensorFlow is an open-source machine learning platform developed by Google. It provides a wide range of tools and resources for creating and training AI models, including pre-built models and tutorials.

PyTorch: https://pytorch.org/

PyTorch is another popular open-source machine learning platform that provides an easy-to-use interface for building AI models. It's particularly well-suited for deep learning and natural language processing (NLP) tasks.

Scikit-learn: https://scikit-learn.org/

Scikit-learn is a machine learning library for Python that provides a variety of algorithms for classification, regression, clustering, and dimensionality reduction. It's a great choice if you're just getting started with machine learning and want to experiment with different algorithms.

Coursera Machine Learning Course:
https://www.coursera.org/learn/machine-learning

This online course by Andrew Ng provides a comprehensive introduction to machine learning concepts and techniques. It covers everything from linear regression to neural networks and deep learning, and includes hands-on programming assignments to help you apply what you've learned.

TensorFlow Tutorials: https://www.tensorflow.org/tutorials

The TensorFlow website provides a variety of tutorials on how to use TensorFlow for different machine learning tasks, including image classification, natural language processing, and recommendation systems.

PyTorch Tutorials: https://pytorch.org/tutorials/

The PyTorch website also provides a variety of tutorials on how to use PyTorch for different machine learning tasks, including image and text classification, language modeling, and generative models.

✓ **Fine-tuning the model for better results**

Once you have created and trained your AI model, the next step is to fine-tune it for better results. Fine-tuning refers to the process of adjusting the parameters of your model to improve its accuracy or performance on a specific task. Here are some steps you can follow to fine-tune your AI model:

- **Evaluate your model**: Before you start fine-tuning your model, you should first evaluate its performance on your test data. This will help you identify areas where the model is performing poorly and where you need to focus your efforts.

- **Adjust hyperparameters**: Hyperparameters are the settings of your model that are not learned during training, such as the learning rate, the number of layers, or the number of neurons in each layer. Adjusting these hyperparameters can significantly impact your model's performance, so it's important to experiment with different settings to find the best combination.

- **Regularize your model**: Regularization refers to techniques that prevent your model from overfitting to your training data, which can result in poor performance on new data. Some common regularization techniques include dropout, L1 and L2 regularization, and early stopping.

- **Use transfer learning**: Transfer learning is a technique where you start with a pre-trained model and then fine-tune it on your own data. This can be a powerful way to improve the performance of your model, particularly if you don't have a large amount of training data.

- **Ensembling:** Ensembling refers to combining the predictions of multiple models to improve their overall accuracy. This can be done in several ways, such as by averaging the predictions of multiple models or by using a more sophisticated technique such as a gradient boosting or a neural network ensemble.

- **Monitor and evaluate the performance**: Once you have fine-tuned your model, it's important to continue monitoring its performance to ensure it continues to deliver accurate results. You should also regularly evaluate the model on new data to ensure it remains effective in real-world scenarios.

✓ **Deploying the AI model on a website**

Once you have created and fine-tuned your AI model, the next step is to deploy it on a website. Here are some steps you can follow to deploy your AI model on a website:

- **Choose a web hosting service**: There are many web hosting services available that you can use to host your website, such as AWS, Google Cloud, and Microsoft Azure. Choose a web hosting service that suits your needs and budget.

- **Choose a web development framework**: There are many web development frameworks available that you can use to build your website, such as Flask, Django, and Node.js. Choose a web development framework that suits your skills and experience.

- **Integrate your AI model with your website**: You can integrate your AI model with your website by using a web API or by embedding the model directly in your website code. If you are using a web API, you can use a RESTful API to communicate between your website and your model. If you are embedding the model directly in your website code, you can use a Python library such as TensorFlow.js or Keras.js to load the model and make predictions in the browser.

- **Test your website**: Once you have integrated your AI model with your website, you should test your website thoroughly to ensure that everything is working correctly. Test your website on different browsers and devices to ensure that it is responsive and user-friendly.

- **Deploy your website**: Once you are satisfied that your website is working correctly, you can deploy it to your web hosting service. Follow the instructions provided by your web hosting service to deploy your website and make it accessible to the public.

Here are some resources that can help you deploy your AI model on a website:

1. **Deploying Machine Learning Models with Flask:** This article provides a step-by-step guide to deploying a machine learning model with Flask, a Python web development framework. https://towardsdatascience.com/deploying-a-machine-learning-model-as-a-rest-api-4a03b865c166

2. **Building a Website with TensorFlow.js**: This tutorial shows you how to build a website with TensorFlow.js, a JavaScript library that allows you to load and run machine learning models in the browser. https://www.tensorflow.org/js/tutorials/deploying_tfjs_models_on_web

3. **Deploying a Machine Learning Model on AWS**: This article provides a comprehensive guide to deploying a

machine learning model on AWS, a cloud hosting service. https://towardsdatascience.com/deploying-a-machine-learning-model-on-aws-ec2-instance-part-1-9050e2c320b6

4. **Deploying a Machine Learning Model on Google Cloud**: This tutorial shows you how to deploy a machine learning model on Google Cloud, a cloud hosting service. https://cloud.google.com/solutions/deploying-machine-learning-models

Developing an AI Website

Website development technologies refer to the different tools and frameworks used to create and maintain websites. Some of the commonly used website development technologies include:

1. **HTML (Hypertext Markup Language):** A standard markup language used to create web pages and web applications.

2. **CSS (Cascading Style Sheets):** A style sheet language used to describe the look and formatting of a document written in HTML.

3. **JavaScript:** A programming language used to add dynamic and interactive features to web pages.

4. **Server-side languages:** Programming languages such as PHP, Python, and Ruby used to build web applications that run on the server.

5. **Content Management Systems (CMS):** Platforms such as WordPress, Drupal, and Joomla used to create, manage, and publish digital content on the web.

6. **Front-end frameworks**: pre-built libraries of HTML, CSS, and JavaScript such as React, Angular, and Vue used to build user interfaces.

7. **Back-end frameworks**: pre-built libraries and tools for server-side programming such as Express.js (for Node.js), Django (for Python), and Ruby on Rails (for Ruby).

✓ **Integrating the AI model into the website**

Integrating the AI model into a website involves connecting the model to the website's backend and creating the necessary frontend components to interact with the AI model. Here are the steps involved in integrating an AI model into a website:

- **Choose a web development framework**: Select a web development framework that supports the programming language used to develop the AI model. For example, if the AI model was developed using Python, Flask or Django can be used as the web development framework.

- **Expose the model as an API:** The AI model should be exposed as a RESTful API (Application Programming Interface) so that it can be called from the website's backend.

- **Create API endpoints**: Create endpoints in the website's backend code that can receive data from the website's frontend and call the AI model API.

- **Develop frontend components**: Develop the necessary frontend components that allow users to interact with the AI model. For example, if the AI model is a chatbot, a frontend component can be created to display the chatbot and allow users to chat with it.

- **Implement AI functionality**: Integrate the AI functionality into the website's frontend and backend code. For example, if the AI model is a recommendation engine, implement the necessary logic in the backend code to retrieve recommendations from the AI model and display them on the website's frontend.

- **Test the integration**: Thoroughly test the integration to ensure that the AI model is working as expected and that there are no issues with the website's functionality.

Here is a helpful link that provides a tutorial on integrating an AI model into a website using Flask as the web development framework:

https://towardsdatascience.com/build-a-chatbot-with-pythons-flask-framework-and-dialogflow-68a1d16b166d

This tutorial walks through the process of building a chatbot using Google's Dialogflow and integrating it into a Flask web application. While the tutorial focuses on chatbots, the same principles can be applied to other types of AI models.

Additionally, here is a link to another tutorial on integrating an AI model into a website using TensorFlow.js:

https://www.tensorflow.org/js/tutorials/deployment/hosting_your_tfjs_model_on_the_web

This tutorial covers the process of training an image classification model using TensorFlow.js and then deploying it to a website using JavaScript. While the tutorial is specific to image classification models, the same principles can be applied to other types of models.

✓ Creating a user interface for the AI-powered features

When creating a user interface for AI-powered features, it's important to keep the user experience in mind. Here are some steps you can follow to create an effective user interface for your AI-powered website:

- **Define the user flow**: Identify the user journey and what they need to accomplish on your website. Define the different steps a user will take to achieve their goals and what they will see on each page.

- **Design the interface**: Based on the user flow, design the interface for each page, keeping in mind the user experience. Use clear and concise language and make sure the design is intuitive and easy to use.

- **Incorporate the AI features**: Determine where and how the AI-powered features will be integrated into the user interface. Consider using interactive elements such as buttons, sliders, or chatbots to provide a more engaging user experience.

- **Test the interface**: Test the user interface with real users to ensure it is easy to use and understand. Gather feedback and make necessary improvements.

- **Continuously iterate**: As your AI model improves or your users' needs change, continue to iterate and improve your user interface to keep up with the evolving landscape.

When creating a user interface for your AI-powered website, it's also important to consider accessibility for users with disabilities. Ensure that the website design and functionality meet the Web Content Accessibility Guidelines (WCAG) to make the website accessible to a wider audience.

✓ **Testing and refining the AI website**

Once you have integrated your AI model into your website and designed a user interface for the AI-powered features, it's time to test and refine your AI website. Here are some steps you can follow:

- **Test the AI model:** Before testing the website, it's important to test the AI model separately to ensure it is performing as expected. Use a validation dataset to evaluate the model's accuracy, precision, recall, and F1 score. Make necessary adjustments to improve the model's performance.

- **Conduct user testing:** Test the website with real users to gather feedback on the user experience, user interface, and AI-powered features. Identify areas where users may be struggling or encountering errors and make necessary improvements.

- **Analyze user behavior**: Use website analytics tools to gather data on user behavior, such as which pages are most frequently visited and which features are most frequently used. Use this data to refine the user interface and improve the AI-powered features.

- **Optimize website speed and performance**: Ensure that the website loads quickly and is optimized for performance to provide a smooth user experience. Use tools such as Google PageSpeed Insights to identify areas where the website can be optimized for speed and performance.

- **Continuously monitor and improve**: As your website receives more traffic and user feedback, continue to monitor and improve the AI-powered features and user interface to provide the best possible experience for your users.

Here are some helpful resources for testing and refining an AI website:

1. "The Ultimate Guide to Testing AI Applications": This article from the AI consulting firm Emerj provides a comprehensive overview of testing strategies for AI applications, including website development. It covers topics such as unit testing, integration testing, regression testing, and more.

Link: https://emerj.com/ai-executive-guides/the-ultimate-guide-to-testing-ai-applications/

2. "10 Best Practices for Testing and Debugging AI Applications": This article from Forbes provides tips and best practices for testing and debugging AI applications. It covers topics such as data validation, model validation, and testing in production.

Link: https://www.forbes.com/sites/cognitiveworld/2019/03/22/10-best-practices-for-testing-and-debugging-ai-applications/?sh=3e32ebca7469

3. "Testing Machine Learning Models": This article from the machine learning platform Databricks provides a detailed overview of testing strategies for machine learning models, including techniques for evaluating model accuracy and identifying errors.

Link: https://databricks.com/glossary/testing-machine-learning-models

4. "Testing AI Systems - A Comprehensive Guide": This article from the software testing company Testim.io provides a detailed guide to testing AI systems, including techniques for testing natural language processing (NLP) models and computer vision models.

Link: https://www.testim.io/blog/testing-ai-systems-a-comprehensive-guide/

Best Practices for AI Website Development

✓ **Ethical considerations in AI website development**

Ethics is an important aspect of any technology, and AI is no exception. AI website developers need to consider several ethical considerations when developing AI-powered websites. Some of the key ethical considerations include:

- **Transparency**: AI models can sometimes make decisions that are difficult to explain. It's important to ensure that users can understand the decision-making process of the AI model and have access to information about how their data is being used.

- **Fairness**: AI models should be designed in a way that is fair and unbiased towards all users, regardless of their race, gender, or other personal characteristics.

- **Privacy**: AI models should be designed in a way that protects user privacy and prevents the misuse of user data.

- **Accountability**: Developers should be accountable for the decisions made by AI models and take responsibility for any negative outcomes that may result from their use.

- **Safety**: AI models should be designed in a way that ensures the safety of users and prevents harm.

✓ Best practices for data privacy and security

Data privacy and security are crucial considerations for any website development project, especially those involving AI. Here are some best practices for ensuring data privacy and security in AI website development:

- **Data Encryption**: Use encryption methods like SSL/TLS to secure the communication between the server and the client. This will protect the data from being intercepted and read by unauthorized individuals.

- **Secure Database:** Store user data and other sensitive information in secure databases that are designed to protect against unauthorized access. Implement access controls and authentication methods to ensure that only authorized users can access the data.

- **Regular Data Backups**: It's essential to regularly backup your data to protect against data loss due to hardware failure or cyber attacks.

- **Regular Security Audits**: Conduct regular security audits to identify vulnerabilities and fix them before they can be exploited by attackers.

- **Privacy Policy**: Ensure that your website has a privacy policy that outlines how user data is collected, stored, and used. Make sure that the policy is clear, concise, and easily understandable by users.

- **Compliance**: Ensure that your website complies with all relevant data protection laws, such as GDPR, CCPA, or HIPAA, depending on your industry and location.

✓ **Monitoring and maintaining the AI model and website**

Monitoring and maintaining an AI model and website is a crucial aspect of ensuring their optimal performance and security. Here are some best practices:

1. **Regular monitoring**: It's important to regularly monitor the AI model and website for any issues or anomalies.

This can be done using various tools and techniques such as logging, alerts, and analytics.

2. **Performance optimization**: AI models can become slow or inefficient over time due to changes in the data, algorithm, or hardware. Regular performance optimization can help improve the speed and accuracy of the model.

3. **Security updates**: Websites and AI models can be vulnerable to security threats such as hacking, data breaches, and malware attacks. Regular security updates and patches can help prevent such issues.

4. **Data backups**: It's important to have a backup of the data used in the AI model to ensure that it can be restored in case of any data loss or corruption.

5. **Version control**: Version control is crucial in maintaining the AI model as it helps to keep track of the changes made to the model over time. This can be done using various tools such as Git.

6. **Documentation**: Proper documentation of the AI model and website can help ensure their maintainability, reusability, and scalability. It can also help in troubleshooting and debugging issues.

7. **Compliance with regulations**: Websites and AI models must comply with various regulations such as GDPR, CCPA, HIPAA, etc. It's important to ensure that the AI model and website are compliant with all relevant regulations.

Here are some helpful links for more information:

- "Best practices for maintaining machine learning models" by Google: https://developers.google.com/machine-learning/guides/rules-of-ml

- "Best practices for securing AI and machine learning systems" by IBM: https://www.ibm.com/blogs/ibm-training/best-practices-for-securing-ai-and-machine-learning-systems/

- "Best practices for data privacy and security in AI" by Forbes: https://www.forbes.com/sites/forbestechcouncil/2021/04/29/best-practices-for-data-privacy-and-security-in-ai/?sh=27b117f4414a

- "Maintaining your AI models in production: A guide to MLOps" by Microsoft: https://azure.microsoft.com/en-us/solutions/machine-learning/mlops/

Future of AI Website Development

Artificial intelligence (AI) has been transforming the way websites are developed and managed, and its impact is only going to increase in the coming years. As AI technology continues to advance, it is expected to bring about major changes in the way websites are built, maintained, and improved.

In this section, we will discuss some of the emerging trends in AI website development, potential future applications of AI in website development, and the challenges and opportunities that lie ahead for AI website developers.

✓ Emerging Trends in AI Website Development

Natural Language Processing (NLP)

One of the most promising areas of AI website development is NLP, which involves teaching machines to understand and interpret human language. This technology has the potential to revolutionize the way websites are designed and maintained. For example, chatbots that are powered by NLP can interact with website visitors in a natural and conversational way, answering questions and providing support.

Personalization

AI technology is also making it easier to personalize website experiences for individual users. By analyzing user data such as search history and behavior, AI algorithms can create personalized content and recommendations for each user. This helps to increase engagement and improve the user experience, ultimately leading to increased conversions and sales.

Voice User Interface (VUI)

With the increasing popularity of smart speakers and voice assistants, VUI is becoming an important area of AI website development. Websites that are optimized for VUI can be accessed and navigated using voice commands, allowing users to interact with the website in a more natural and intuitive way.

Predictive Analytics

Predictive analytics involves using AI algorithms to analyze data and make predictions about future events or trends. In website development, this technology can be used to predict user behavior, identify trends in website traffic, and improve website performance.

✓ **Potential Future Applications of AI in Website Development**

Augmented Reality (AR)

As AR technology continues to advance, it is expected to play a larger role in website development. AR can be used to create immersive website experiences, allowing users to interact with digital content in the real world.

Visual Search

Visual search technology allows users to search for products and information using images instead of text. This technology is becoming increasingly popular, and it is expected to play a larger role in website development in the future.

Automated Content Creation

AI algorithms can already generate basic content such as news articles and product descriptions. In the future, it is possible that AI will be able to generate more complex content such as video and audio content, further reducing the need for human intervention in the content creation process.

✓ **Challenges and Opportunities for AI Website Developers**

Ethical Considerations

As AI technology becomes more powerful, it is important for website developers to consider the ethical implications of their work. Issues such as data privacy and algorithmic bias must be carefully considered and addressed.

Skill Development

As AI technology continues to advance, it is essential for website developers to keep their skills up to date. Developers must learn how to work with new tools and technologies, and stay up to date with the latest developments in the field.

Security

As websites become increasingly reliant on AI technology, it is important to ensure that these systems are secure and protected from hackers and other malicious actors.

Human Oversight

While AI technology has the potential to automate many tasks involved in website development, it is important to maintain a balance between human and machine involvement. Human oversight is necessary to ensure that AI systems are working as intended, and to address any issues that may arise.

Conclusion

In this book, we have explored the world of AI website development, including the types of AI models used in website development, the process of creating and training an AI model, and best practices for integrating AI into a website. We have also discussed ethical considerations, data privacy and security, monitoring, and maintaining AI models and websites.

We have seen that AI has already revolutionized website development, enabling developers to create more personalized, efficient, and engaging websites. With AI, websites can be optimized for search engines, analyze user behavior, and provide intelligent recommendations to users. In the future, AI will continue to transform website development, with new applications and possibilities emerging every day.

However, with great power comes great responsibility. AI developers must be aware of the ethical considerations involved in AI development, including bias, transparency, and privacy. They must also ensure that their AI models and websites are secure and protect user data.

The future of AI website development is exciting, but it requires careful consideration of ethical and security implications. By following best practices and staying up-to-date on emerging trends, developers can create AI-powered websites that provide value to users while protecting their privacy and security.

The book covered the following key points in AI website development:

- **Introduction to AI**: The book started by providing an introduction to AI and its various subfields.

- **AI in Website Development**: The book then explored the various applications of AI in website development.

- **Types of AI Models**: The book discussed the different types of AI models that can be used in website development, including supervised learning, unsupervised learning, and reinforcement learning.

- **Creating and Training AI Models**: The book provided a step-by-step guide for creating and training an AI model for website development.

- **Fine-tuning AI Models**: The book also discussed the process of fine-tuning an AI model for better results.

- **Deploying AI Models on a Website**: The book explained how to deploy an AI model on a website.

- **Developing an AI Website**: The book then discussed the various technologies used in website development and how to integrate an AI model into a website.

- **User Interface for AI-Powered Features**: The book explained how to create a user interface for AI-powered features.

- **Testing and refining the AI Website**: The book also provided guidance on how to test and refine the AI website.

- **Ethical Considerations**: The book discussed the ethical considerations in AI website development and best practices for data privacy and security.

- **Monitoring and Maintaining AI Model and Website**: Finally, the book provided guidance on how to monitor and maintain the AI model and website.

The rise of artificial intelligence is the great story of our time. These technologies are not only transforming the way we live and work but also changing the way we interact with the world around us."

- Fei-Fei Li, computer scientist and AI expert